CRIME SCENE SCIENCE

CRIME SCENE INVESTIGATION

By Lorraine Jean Hopping

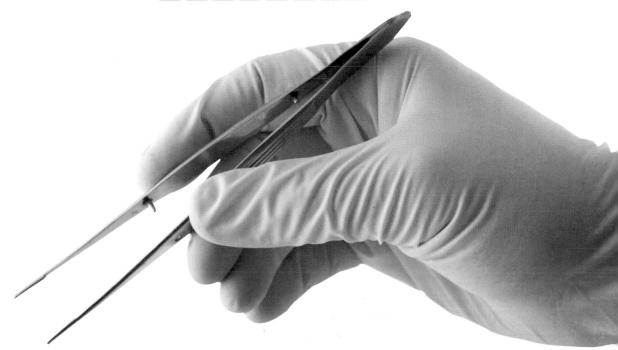

First published in Great Britain in 2007 by ticktock Media Ltd,
2 Orchard Business Centre, North Farm Road, Tunbridge Wells, Kent, TN2 3XF

ISBN-13: 978-1-84696-320-9 pbk

Printed in China

Editor: Ruth Owen
Designer: Vicky Crichton
Picture Researcher: Lizzie Knowles

ACKNOWLEDGEMENTS
The author and publisher extend a big thank you to Detectives Nichol Jennings, Ann Marie
Ziska, and Mike Smith in Cleveland; C.S.I. Sharon Plotkin and Detective Christine Kruse-
Feldstein in Florida; Detective Don Hrycyk in Los Angeles; and Dr. Diane France of NecroSearch
in Colorado for their contributed time and wisdom.

With thanks to science educator Suzy Gazlay for her insightful thoughts and comments.

Thank you to Jean Coppendale and Indexing Specialists (UK) Ltd.

PICTURE CREDITS

t = top, b = bottom, c = centre, l = left, r = right, OFC = outside front cover, OBC = outside back cover

Alamy: 25b. Picture © BLUESTAR®: 27t, 27cl, 27b. BrandXpictures: 43b. Corbis: 22t, 24b. Courtesy of Christine K. Feldstein
and Sharon L. Plotkin CSI: OFCr, 10t, 14t, 15t, 15b, 18t, 19tl, 19tr, 21tl, 21tr, 24t, 26b, 29all, 33b, 37b, 41t, 45tl, 45tr, 45c. Detective Don Hrycyk
LAPD art theft detail: 36b, 37tl, 37tr, 38/39. Courtesy of Nichol Jennings: 16b, 17c, 17b, 40t. Mikael Karlsson/ arrestingimages.com: 14b, 17t, 19b,
22b, 33c. Rex Features: 4b, 30/31, 42c, 42b, 43t. Shutterstock: OFC Background, 1, 3, 4t, 5t, 5c, 6b, 7 all, 8, 10br, 11 all, 12t, 12b, 15b, 16t, 18c,
21b, 23t, 28l, 32all, 34t, 36tl, 36tc, 36tr, 38b, 39bl, 39br, 42tl, 42tc, 42tr, 44 all, 45tl, OBC Background, OBC. Science Photo Library: OFCc
(original), 6t, 9, 13t, 23b, 28r, 34b, 35, 41b. Superstock 40b. ticktock Media Archive: OFCl, 5b, 10bl, 12c, 25tl, 25tc, 25tr, 33t, 39t, 99c.
www.evidentcrimescene.com: 27c x 4.

Every effort has been made to trace the copyright holders, and we apologise in advance for any unintentional omissions.
We would be pleased to insert the appropriate acknowledgements in any subsequent edition of this publication.

CONTENTS

POLICE LINE DO NOT CROSS

Observation is step one in working a crime scene. It's a science thinking skill that takes two eyes, a brain, and any number of simple to high-tech tools.

You can catch a criminal with your hands. Police officers do it all the time; they make arrests and haul suspects off to jail. You can catch a criminal with your mind. Detectives use brain power, along with dogged legwork, to track down, "Who did it?" You can also catch a criminal with science.

The *Crime Scene Science* series explains how to do it. This book spotlights the crime scene. It features real crime scene investigations, so, be warned, that spotlight might seem a little bright and glaring at times!

The crime scene boss

The boss of a crime scene is the crime scene investigator (C.S.I.), an umbrella term for a range of job titles. Whatever the specific label, he or she is the person in charge of everyone and everything at the scene: every footprint, every stray hair, every speck of blood. (Everything, that is, except the dead body, if there is one. Corpses belong to a doctor called a forensic pathologist.)

Working alone or with a team, the C.S.I. processes the scene. Slowly and thoroughly, step by careful step, he or she uncovers evidence, photographs it, and collects it. Unlike some witnesses and suspects, this collection – the physical evidence – doesn't lie. It tells the true crime story to those who know how to listen.

The C.S.I. interprets the physical evidence to figure out: "What happened here?" Detectives rely on the answer, and other facts, to solve the crime.

The rule of contact

Forensic means having to do with evidence in an investigation, which can be a crime case,

Don't believe everything you see on TV shows like *CSI: Crime Scene Investigation*. Unlike real investigators, the writers are free to make up 'science' (science fiction, really) to solve a case in a fast-paced, entertaining hour.

Are you thinking 'Blood! Murder!'? Not so fast. Investigators keep an open mind and consider all possibilities. Maybe that 'blood' is ketchup. Maybe the 'murder' was an accident.

an accident, or a natural disaster. At the centre of a criminal investigation is the number one rule of forensic science: *every contact leaves a trace*. A criminal who comes in contact with a victim leaves behind and takes away physical evidence. The same is true for a criminal and a location – a burglar in a store for instance. With contact, there's always a transfer of evidence.

Imagine you're in a crime scene. What proof of your presence will you leave behind? What will you take with you? Drawing a blank? Think tiny: as you read this, your body is shedding hairs and dead skin cells. Oil from your fingertips is forming fingerprints on surfaces (like the cover of this book).

Loose fibres from your clothing are dropping to the floor or sticking to the furniture. Likewise, dust and fibres from a carpet or a chair could be sticking to you.

To seek out evidence, no matter how tiny, a C.S.I. relies on observation – a thinking skill that goes way beyond looking. Observing is about noticing details and deciding what's important, and what's not. It's about asking lots of questions: how did this get here? What's out of place? What's missing from the scene? What doesn't make sense?

Here's how crime scene investigators use science, technology, and brain power to tell the true story behind a crime.

Evidence bags are tightly sealed to prevent anyone from messing with the contents. To examine those contents, an investigator cuts open the side but leaves the seal intact as proof that it was never broken.

THINK LIKE A CRIME SCIENTIST

- **What do you observe?**
Look around! Seek out and think about details: what's out of place or missing? What doesn't make sense?

- **What can you infer?**
An inference is an indirect observation. If you observe fingerprints on a glass, you can infer someone touched the glass, even though you didn't see it happen.

- **What is the evidence?**
Evidence is proof of a fact. It can be physical (objects like a weapon or blood) or statements made by witnesses.

- **What does the evidence mean?**
Interpret the evidence and then propose a hypothesis (an idea) of what happened. Then test that idea against all the known facts.

- **What's your theory?**
If the facts fit, you have a theory of the crime, an explanation of who, what, when, where, why, and how.

5

A Scene Of Crime Officer (SOCO), in the UK, examines a bullet hole at a travel agency that was robbed. The time right after a crime is called the 'Golden Hour' because that's when the most and the freshest evidence can be collected.

Criminals don't want to get caught. That sounds obvious, doesn't it? Even so, keep that 'evident' fact in mind while you think about crime scenes – where they are, what's in them, and how to 'read' them for the true story of, "What happened here?"

What's a crime scene?

A crime scene is any place where evidence is found. It might be the scene of the crime – the location where a crime took place. In the next chapter, you'll read how a detective investigating the scene of a shooting 'pressed a button' to solve the crime.

A crime scene doesn't have to be the scene of a crime. It could be the hangout of a suspect or where a crime was planned. It could be the getaway car in a drive-by shooting, or the pond where a robber tossed a gun. It could be a suitcase holding an unexploded bomb or the telephone on which a kidnapper asked for money. In the case of convicted murderer Stella Nickell, it was a bookshelf. (See ON THE CASE: A Textbook Case, page 7.)

The crime scene is anywhere that evidence lurks. And lurks is a good word because remember, criminals don't want anyone to find that evidence.

A team investigates the scene of a crime, which is the place where a crime happened – in this case, a fatal shooting. A crime scene is anywhere evidence is found, such as the home of the shooter.

ON THE CASE:

A TEXTBOOK CASE

Stella Nickell of Auburn, Washington, sits in prison with a 99-year sentence for murdering her husband. Three ordinary items recovered at crime scenes helped put her there.

In the trailer where she lived, investigators found two aspirin bottles and a fish tank. The other crime scene was a library bookshelf.

Here's what happened:

On 6 June, 1986, Bruce Nickell died suddenly. The forensic pathologist said the cause was a lung condition. But then, five days later, a woman named Sue Snow died suddenly, too. Lab tests showed that she had been poisoned. The poison, cyanide, had been added to aspirin capsules.

Stella Nickell called the police and told them that her husband had swallowed the same brand of aspirin moments before he died. She believed her husband had been poisoned, too. She was right: her trailer had not one, but two bottles of tainted aspirin. A lab test detected cyanide in a sample of Bruce Nickell's blood. The manner of death was changed from 'natural' to 'murder'.

FINGER OF GUILT

If Stella Nickell was the killer, why did she report her crime to police? Why not let them keep thinking her husband's death was natural? Whatever the reason, physical evidence pointed two fingers of guilt at her.

In the Auburn library, an agent from the Federal Bureau of Investigation (F.B.I.) found a book about poisons called 'Deadly Harvest'. Another book, 'Human Poisoning,' was overdue. Nickell had checked out both books before her husband's death. In 'Deadly Harvest,' investigators found 84 of her fingerprints, most of them in the chapter about cyanide.

There was another clue in the aspirin. Along with cyanide, it contained crystals of a chemical used in fish tanks. The killer had mixed the aspirin-cyanide powder in the same bowl used to crush those crystals. Stella Nickell had a fish tank. A local pet store owner remembered her buying the crystals, although none were found in her trailer.

AN INSURANCE PAYOUT

F.B.I. investigators believed she poisoned her husband. Then, after his death was incorrectly ruled 'natural,' she wanted it changed to 'murder' in order to collect more life insurance money. So she placed bottles of tainted aspirin on store shelves. Sue Snow, tragically, bought one. Her death gave Nickell an excuse to call the police and reopen her husband's case. In 1982, a similar case of aspirin poisoning went unsolved. Nickell thought her crime would, too. Instead, crime scene investigators turned it into a 'textbook case' of murder.

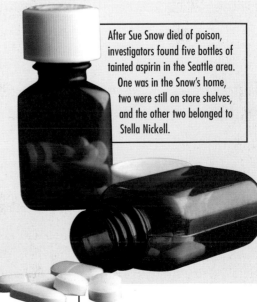

After Sue Snow died of poison, investigators found five bottles of tainted aspirin in the Seattle area. One was in the Snow's home, two were still on store shelves, and the other two belonged to Stella Nickell.

ON THE CASE:

A NEEDLE IN A HAIR STACK

In August 1974, a 25-year-old photographer named Michele Wallace disappeared in the Colorado Rockies. Thirty airplanes and more than 400 ground searchers couldn't find her. A week later, her dog Okee, turned up at a ranch. Her car, her camping gear, and her camera ended up in the hot-fingered hands of Roy Melanson.

Where was Michele Wallace? Melanson admitted he stole her things but denied harming her. Detectives suspected otherwise, but, without a body or other evidence, they had no case.

BRAIDS AND A BRUSH

Five years later, in 1979, a hiker on a steep, wooded mountain found a piece of scalp with two long, braids of hair. Forensic scientists couldn't prove they belonged to Michele Wallace, and no other clues turned up. Then, in 1989, Wallace's hairbrush was discovered in an evidence bag that had been stored away. A crime lab matched the braids to samples of hair from the brush.

The question became: where was the grave? In 1991, Detective Kathy Young asked NecroSearch to hunt for it.

The young photographer had been missing for 17 years. Diane France, a forensic anthropologist or 'bone detective,' says that, over time, human remains are 'scattered by gravity, wind, rain, and scavengers'. They're also, 'covered by leaves, pine needles, and debris'. In other words, this search would be tougher than finding a needle in a haystack.

Fortunately, there were pine needles stuck in the braids. NecroSearch botanist Vickey Trammell identified them as belonging to trees that grow above a certain elevation. Because the hair and needles weren't sun-bleached, the team began the search on the high, north side of the mountain – the shady side.

AT LAST A CRIME SCENE

Hours of hard work turned up nothing but mosquito bites. Then, on a rest break, a NecroSearch naturalist spotted what looked like a large, white 'mushroom'.

The treeline of a mountain is the altitude at which the climate becomes too cold and dry for plant growth. Only a few kinds of trees can survive near that high mark. Needles from one of them led investigators to a Rocky Mountain crime scene.

It turned out to be a cranium – the top part of a skull. The team had a crime scene!

A shoulder-to-shoulder search on hands and knees turned up more scattered bones – six ribs, part of a backbone, 25 foot bones, and other evidence. A gold tooth matched the dental records of Michele Wallace. The bones were consistent with her age, sex, and height. In 1993, Roy Melanson was convicted of murder and sentenced to life in prison.

A team takes photographs, makes sketches, and writes detailed notes to document exactly how a body was found.

They hide it, or disguise it, or destroy it, or make it look as if it belongs to someone else. So where does evidence lurk? In the case of homicide, one person killing another, the most important evidence to find is the corpse.

Hidden graves

NecroSearch is a group of about 40 experts based in Colorado, USA, who look for hidden crime scenes around the world. These scientists, detectives, criminalists, and other crime fighters pool their skills to find clandestine graves – places where murderers hide their victims. They scour fields, mountain sides, woods, empty mine shafts, the bottoms of lakes, and other likely hiding spots.

In an area that can stretch hundreds of kilometres, how do they know where to look? Remember: killers don't want to get caught. They especially don't want to get caught red-handed – with a dead body in their possession. So they often wait for the darkness of night or wrap the body in a carpet, rubbish bags, or other containers. Then, they try to dump it in an out-of-the-way place without being seen. But not too far away. The longer the cover-up takes, the greater the chance of getting caught, so killers are usually in a hurry.

A rotting corpse releases some 400 chemicals into the air and ground. Dogs are trained to sniff out the scent of human death in the search for clandestine graves and victims of natural disasters. Search and rescue dogs learn to follow the chemical trail of living humans.

Human remains become scattered by scavengers such as coyotes (below right), foxes, bears, cougars, and birds.

NecroSearch uses those facts to narrow the search for a clandestine grave. Think about it: would a murderer dump a body close to or far from a road? Uphill or downhill? Buried deep, buried shallow, or in the open? Some place familiar or some place unknown to the killer?

A general rule is: whatever's fastest and easiest, and away from prying eyes. That means probably close to a roadside, since bodies are heavy to carry. Downhill from the road is more likely than uphill, for the same reason. A shallow grave or unburied means less time and effort for digging.

Diane France, the president of the group,

Ground penetrating radar (GPR) allows searchers to look underground without digging up (and ruining) a crime scene. The machine beams a radar signal into the ground. Buried objects absorb and reflect the energy in different ways. The differences are measured and mapped by computer.

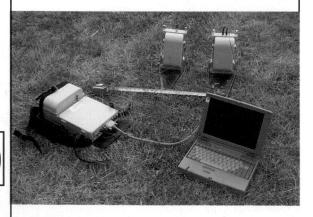

says that, in three out of four NecroSearch cases, the clandestine grave is on land the suspect owns, controls, or knows well. Why risk getting lost? Or running into a stranger?

Where's the body?

After narrowing the search area, finding the grave involves observation, science and technology, along with a little luck. (See ON THE CASE: A Needle in a Hair Stack, page 8.) Naturally, the team looks for soil that's been disturbed. But a freshly dug grave doesn't look freshly dug for long. Most searches have to go into finer detail.

NecroSearch botanists (plant experts) look for a patch of vegetation that has changed, since bodies nourish plants as part of the cycle of life. Biologists seek out signs of scavengers and decomposers, animals that feed on dead organisms.

The most-requested NecroSearch experts are the geophysicists, scientists who can search underground without digging. They use remote-sensing instruments, like ground-penetrating radar (GPR) or a magnetometer that senses magnetic fields in the soil. An odd spot in the magnetic pattern could mean earth that's been dug up and replaced. Other instruments detect soil density (compactness), gases, and infrared light, which is a clue to the heat given off by decomposing bodies. (Infrared light, unlike visible light, is a form of electromagnetic energy that we can't see.)

POLICE LINE DO NOT CROSS

If any trace of a body or a grave is found, the area instantly becomes a crime scene. It's roped off and a walkline is created. A walkline is a single, narrow path, cleared of evidence that everyone uses to enter and exit the crime scene. That way, no one accidentally tramples evidence. The scene is processed slowly and carefully, using in-depth techniques described in Chapter 3.

Getting the call

NecroSearch has more misses than hits; it's hard to pinpoint a tiny grave in kilometres of wilderness. Other crime scenes come to light quickly with a phone call. A victim or witness dials 999 emergency to summon first responders – police officers, a fire crew, or an ambulance. After taking care of people in need and arresting suspects, the officers seal off the area with bright, yellow tape or barriers. They call in detectives, who request a crime scene investigator.

Bluebottle flies are often the first in a parade of insects to lay eggs on a rotting corpse. Their eggs hatch into larvae (below) in a few days to a week, depending on the temperature. Therefore, the presence of larvae on a corpse is a clue to time of death.

Forensic naturalists look for animal traces – footprints, hairs, feathers, and scat – both to locate a hidden grave and to recover missing evidence.

11

Police officers arrest suspects. Police detectives interview witnesses and work to solve the crime.

THE CRIME SCENE TEAM

On small crime cases, such as a burglary, one investigator often processes the whole scene. A large crime scene team can include these and other specialists:

- Police officers and other emergency workers are often the first to arrive. Officers arrest suspects and seal off the scene.

- A crime scene investigator (C.S.I.) takes charge of processing the scene. The specific job title might be forensic scientist, crime scene analyst (C.S.A.) or, in Britain, Scene of Crime Officer (S.O.C.O.).

- A crime scene photographer documents the scene and all the evidence before it's collected.

- Crime scene technicians (C.S.T.s) bag and tag evidence and take it to forensic scientists in the crime lab.

- A forensic pathologist examines the body, if there is one.

- A profiler studies the scene to assess the criminal's mind and motive (reason for his or her behaviour).

- Detectives rely on information and collected evidence from all of the above to solve the crime. They also interview witnesses and suspects and track down clues beyond the scene.

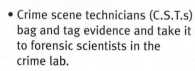

Jumpsuits, booties, and rubber gloves keep investigators from contaminating the scene with traces of themselves — hairs, fingerprints, skin oils, and the like. Gloves and masks protect them from touching or breathing in harmful materials.

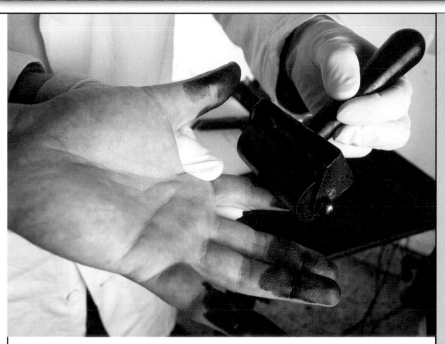

Police take fingerprints of a suspect in order to compare them to prints found at a crime scene. Ink rollers are the cheap but messy method. Electronic fingerprint scanners are more expensive but cleaner and faster.

HELP WANTED!

Forensic Scientist

Duties: Oversee the crime scene team; uncover, collect, and preserve evidence, including trace substances (DNA, fibres, blood, etc.); lift fingerprints; make casts of shoe, tyre, and tool impressions; photograph and sketch crime scenes; log in evidence and request lab tests; work with detectives, medical examiners, and criminalists; write reports; testify in court.

Requirements: A university degree in a science, preferably biology or chemistry. To find out more about a career in forensic science, go to the careers section of http://www.forensic.gov.uk/

Nichol Jennings is an officer assigned to the Crime Scene and Records Unit of the Cleveland, Ohio, Police Department. She goes out on four or five crime scene calls each working day. She says about 95 percent of her cases aren't homicide. By far, most of them are nonviolent – property theft and breaking-and-entering, for example.

Then, on 5 November, 2005, she gets a rare 'code #1 broadcast' – a murder! A female was shot at a residence on East 142nd Street. When Jennings arrives at the address, she notes the names of everyone present for her report. Homicide Detectives Mike Smith and James Rodes are working the case. Police officers have arrested a male suspect.

Jessie Lane, age 74, is in the back of a police car. He keeps babbling that someone shot his wife while he was out in his car, listening to music. He walked into the house, he keeps saying, and found his wife's dead body. It was Lane who made the emergency call.

Detective Smith suspects Lane isn't telling the truth. The elderly man acts and sounds very drunk, the detective notes, and repeats the same story over and over, as if rehearsing a lie. But what will the crime scene evidence say? Nichol Jennings gets set to collect it.

13

A mobile phone at a crime scene has splashes of a dark, red liquid. Is it blood? If so, is it human blood? A C.S.I. has chemical tests to find out for sure.

Every crime scene is different. Yet to avoid mistakes, police departments, the F.B.I., and other agencies have long lists of procedures – steps to follow. One step is to collect fragile or short-lasting evidence right away. That's why, before entering the crime scene at East 142ⁿᵈ Street, Nichol Jennings zeroes in on Jessie Lane.

The suspect

Jennings puts on rubber gloves, removes the suspect from the patrol car, and opens her gunshot residue (GSR) kit. When a gun fires, very tiny specks of powder stick to everything nearby, including the shooter.

It's important to collect those specks from human skin within a couple of hours. After that, the lab test for GSR is useless.

Jennings applies sticky-tape tabs to both

of Jessie Lane's hands, palm-side and back-side. His clothing will be tested for GSR later, at the crime lab.

Jennings notes "suspected blood stains" on the man's hands, jacket, and tee shirt, and photographs them. Until lab tests prove that a non-obvious stain is blood, C.S.I.s think of it as 'suspect' – that is, uncertain.

Next, Jennings begins documenting and observing the scene. She takes pictures of the front of the house and keeps snapping as she makes her way along the perimeter, the outer edge, of the crime scene. She follows a driveway along the side of the house to the back, enters the rear door, and takes in the scene of the crime (see illustration, page 16).

To her left is a small, messy kitchen. The mess looks untidy, more like clutter than the wreckage caused by a struggle. Directly in front of Jennings is a stairway leading to a basement. The body of Rosalind Lane, age 53, is at the bottom of the stairs.

The walkthrough

Crime scene investigators usually don't start with the body. The body belongs to a forensic pathologist, who performs an autopsy, an examination to find the cause of death.

Biological evidence — that's hair, blood, and flesh on a hammer — degrades quickly. But before collecting any evidence, no matter how urgent, it's important to take a close-up photo of the position and pattern.

A C.S.I. applies a gunshot residue (GSR) kit to a hand. A positive test result proves a gun was fired nearby, but a negative one doesn't mean the person is innocent. GSR washes off easily and degrades quickly.

Without touching anything, Jennings continues observing and taking pictures as she walks around the house. She will later log 56 of the colour photos into the evidence book, including wide shots of the entryway, the kitchen, the stairway, and other rooms. Wide shots are a permanent record of where everything was found in relation to everything else. After items are removed or moved, detectives can refer back to these photos.

Jennings takes close-ups of all the obvious evidence, exactly as she finds it. Among other interesting items, she photographs a gun – an Arminius 7–shot .32 revolver, she notes. The weapon is in plain sight on the kitchen counter.

Many investigators still use film cameras to document evidence because digital images are easier to alter. A trial lawyer could suggest objects were added or erased from a digital image, and it would be harder to prove otherwise.

APPROACHING A CRIME SCENE

Before the slow, careful search for evidence, police officers and C.S.I.s have to secure and preserve the crime scene. Here are some of the many steps to follow:

- Think: how did the suspect enter and exit the scene? Look for escape routes and set up a crime scene perimeter, an outer edge, beyond them.

- Keep out all intruders – people, pets, and other animals.

- Call in experts, such as a forensic pathologist, as needed.

- Document the presence of everyone, including their names, fingerprints, and footwear.

- Photograph everything, at every stage, using wide shots and close-ups. "Film is cheap, but evidence is priceless" is the motto.

- Don't touch anything.

- Do a walkthrough. Remember to "look, listen, and smell" – odours can signal the presence of evidence.

- Draw a diagram of the scene.

- Take lots of notes.

- Outline a careful plan of investigation, starting with short-lasting, fragile, and trace evidence.

15

Jessie Lane claimed he was drinking and listening to music in the garage at the time of the shooting. But empty beer cans in the kitchen suggested to detectives that that's where he spent the evening.

The detectives ask Jennings to take pictures of empty beer cans in a bag and a box. She isn't sure why, but she does it. Later, the detectives will point to the cans as evidence that Jessie Lane spent the evening in the house, not in his car, as he kept telling police.

Touching nothing, Jennings takes close-ups of blood spatter in the entryway, of blood swipes along both walls going down the stairwell, and, finally, of the victim. She shoots pictures 'from all possible angles,' as she will write in her report.

A paramedic who checked the body for signs of life, thought the woman had been stabbed in the chest.

To Jennings, the 'stab wound' looks more like an exit wound – a gaping hole where a bullet has left the body. But that's for the forensic pathologist to decide. Her job is to photograph and collect evidence, not to figure out what it means.

Bagging and tagging evidence

After the walkthrough, it's time to 'bag and tag' the evidence. The order of collection is important. It's easy to ruin one piece of evidence while collecting another. For example, if you stuff a shirt into a bag, any trace evidence – hairs, fibres, blood droplets – gets mixed and moved around. A general rule is to collect the tiny stuff first and work up to larger items.

A sketch of the crime scene shows where Nichol Jennings entered (red arrows), where the body was found, and the layout of the house. The gun was fired from the kitchen into the back entryway at the top of the stairs.

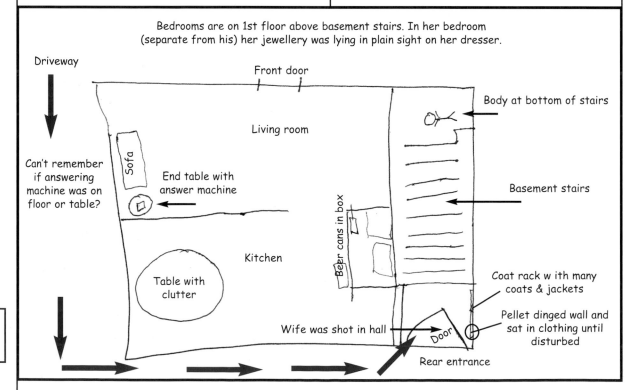

Bedrooms are on 1st floor above basement stairs. In her bedroom (separate from his) her jewellery was lying in plain sight on her dresser.

Driveway

Front door

Body at bottom of stairs

Living room

Sofa

Can't remember if answering machine was on floor or table?

End table with answer machine

Basement stairs

Beer cans in box

Kitchen

Table with clutter

Coat rack with many coats & jackets

Pellet dinged wall and sat in clothing until disturbed

Wife was shot in hall

Door

Rear entrance

A CAREER IN CRIME SCIENCE

PROFILE: JENNINGS & ZISKA – OF THE CRIME SCENE UNIT

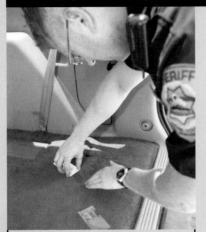

An investigator suspects a body was transported in the back of this vehicle. He's using sticky tape to collect trace evidence – hairs, fibres, and so on.

Nichol Jennings and Ann Marie Ziska are police officers. They graduated from the Police Academy and swore 'to protect and serve' the people of Cleveland, Ohio.

At first, Jennings wanted 'to do it all' – to try every part of police work. She patrolled a street beat and answered calls for help. But after a lot of 'half-stepping,' she figured there had to be a better mousetrap – a better way to catch criminals. She found it when she switched to the Crime Scene and Records Unit, which collects and preserves evidence. "Everything you need is there on the scene," Jennings says. "You just have to find it."

After 15 years on patrol, Ann Marie Ziska joined the same Crime Scene Unit. She graduated from a 10-week training program in forensic science at the National Forensic Academy in Tennessee. But Ziska and Jennings mostly learned on the job, by collecting evidence for detectives at hundreds of crime scenes each year. (The detectives, not the Crime Scene Unit, interpret the evidence and investigate the crimes.)

Besides working crime scenes, Ziska and Jennings also process prisoners – take their fingerprints and photos. Other days, they collect evidence from cars involved in crimes and work in office dispatch, where they send out other officers to crime scenes. Jennings loves being her own boss. "It's my scene," she explains. "I have the freedom to take my time." She can tell everyone to wait, even if it's the mayor or the police chief.

Ziska loves putting herself in the shoes of a criminal. She looks around a scene and asks, "What did he touch? What did he leave behind? What's out of place? Dust it!" By 'dust it,' she means using powders to reveal invisible fingerprints. One fingerprint – sometimes that's all it takes to link a criminal to a crime scene.

"You can catch him!" Jennings says. "When you get the bad guy! It's a rush!"

Nichol Jennings (above) and Ann Marie Ziska (below) log in and process evidence from crime scenes as part of their duties at the Crime Scene and Records Unit.

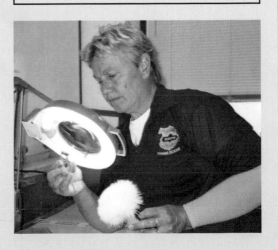

17

Plastic containers are useful for dry evidence, but anything that's wet must be air-dried and placed in paper.

Using swabs on sticks, like the ones at doctor's offices, Jennings picks up three blood samples from the entryway and stairway walls. She lets the swabs dry completely and then places each one in a separate envelope. For all 'bio' – biological samples – it's important to use paper containers, not plastic, to avoid trapping moisture. Moisture allows mould to grow and the material to degrade.

Each evidence container is sealed, dated, and marked with the case number and Jenning's badge number. She is now part of the chain of custody. The next person to handle the evidence – perhaps a forensic scientist or detective – adds his or her name to the list. Everyone who touches the evidence must become part of the chain. There can be no broken links. Every minute of every day, the evidence must be in someone's name. (Why? The answer will become clear in chapter 5.)

The homicide detectives check the .32 revolver in the kitchen and find that it's loaded with one round spent – meaning one bullet fired. They bag the gun for the crime lab, which will examine it for fingerprints and other evidence. The lab will also test-fire it to determine if it's the murder weapon. They compare the pattern of marks on the test slug – the spent round – to a slug found at the scene to see if they match. (It's properly called a slug or a projectile, not a bullet.) Jennings wonders: where is that slug on the scene? She knows exactly where to start looking.

The blood tells the story

A high-speed impact from a gunshot creates very tiny dots of blood spatter. (See THE PHYSICS OF BLOOD STAINS, page 20.) Jennings stands next to the blood spatter in the entryway. It's a small, enclosed space. She figures the shooter (the person who fired the gun) had to be standing in the kitchen. The kitchen counter is less than 3 metres away. She turns around and takes a close look at the door to the entryway. There's a graze mark, like a scrape, perhaps caused by the projectile. She closes the door. Behind it is a jumble of coats, jackets, and sweaters hanging on a rack. She spots a ding mark on the wall, where the projectile hit and bounced off. But there's no hole. The slug isn't in the wall. Jennings grabs the clothes and shakes them.

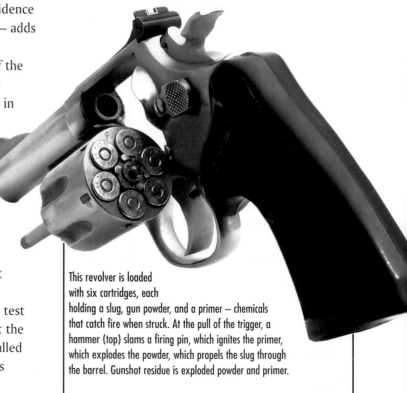

This revolver is loaded with six cartridges, each holding a slug, gun powder, and a primer – chemicals that catch fire when struck. At the pull of the trigger, a hammer (top) slams a firing pin, which ignites the primer, which explodes the powder, which propels the slug through the barrel. Gunshot residue is exploded powder and primer.

C.S.I. EQUIPMENT

Here are a few useful items that a crime scene investigator might carry to the scene.

• MEASURING EQUIPMENT   • MOBILE PHONE   • POLICE RADIO   • TORCH

A C.S.I.'s toolkit contains many different measuring tools and devices: from long tape measures for measuring the crime scene, to equipment that can measure a tiny blood splash.

• MULTI-PURPOSE TOOL (Includes pliers and a screwdriver)

• NOTEBOOK

Out pops the slug! She picks it up and bags this key piece of evidence.

Next, she follows the blood trail down the stairs and tries to picture what happened. Again, interpreting evidence isn't her job – that's what the detectives do. But still, she sees a story in the trail of blood.

At the fourth stair, there are blood swipes on either side on the wall. After being shot in the entryway, Rosalind Lane made it partway down the stairs. Jennings figures the woman clutched her chest wound, sat down on the stair, and touched the walls with both hands. There's a blood stain on a lower step and a mark on the woman's forehead. Jennings pictures her falling forward and hitting her head as she drops to the basement floor.

The grooves on this slug are called rifling. Each type of gun creates a unique rifling pattern as the projectile passes through the barrel.

THE PHYSICS OF BLOOD STAINS

Physics is the science of matter and energy. The matter in these pictures is blood. The energy is about the amount of force used to put it in motion. The volume and velocity (speed and direction) of blood is written in the patterns of stains.

Here are a few common examples:

- In the air, a blood drop is a sphere – a ball. So when gravity causes it to fall straight down, at a 90° angle, it forms a circle when it lands. The lower the angle of impact, the more stretched-out the drop.

- A medium-speed blow creates a spatter pattern with a point of origin and dots that radiate away, like a fan. The farthest dots are more stretched out because they hit the surface at more of an angle.

- A high-speed impact, like a bullet, creates spatter with very tiny drops. As with the medium-speed pattern, the tiny dots are round or stretched out, depending on the angle of impact.

- Criminalists use lasers, pins, or strings, to plot the blood's direction of motion. The point of convergence – where all the lines come together – marks where the injury took place.

- A swipe happens when a bloodied object transfers blood onto a clean surface. A wipe is the opposite – a clean hand smearing a pool of blood, for example.

- Gravity causes blood to flow and pool in low spots. Blood is thicker than water so it flows more slowly, especially as it dries.

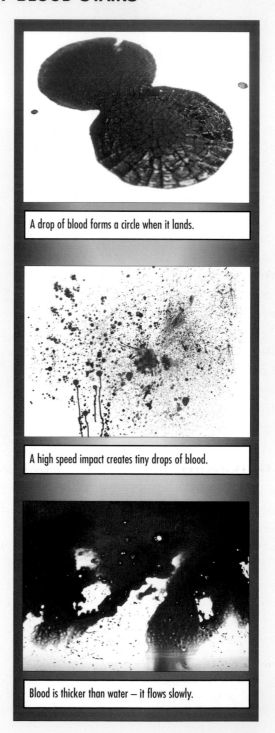

A drop of blood forms a circle when it lands.

A high speed impact creates tiny drops of blood.

Blood is thicker than water – it flows slowly.

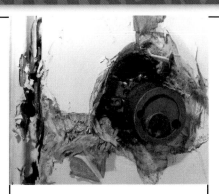

Jessie Lane told police that a burglar entered his home and killed his wife. Yet Nichol Jennings found no sign of a forced entry, like this badly damaged door knob.

When a transport team arrives to take the body to the coroner's office, Jennings asks the men to turn the corpse so that she can take more pictures. On the woman's upper right back, she spots a hole the diameter of a number two pencil. The coroner will later confirm that it's an entrance wound – the spot where the projectile entered the body.

An accidental confession

Meanwhile, Detectives Smith and Rodes have also been looking around for clues. Entrances and exits are always of keen interest. The suspect has to get in and go out somehow.

Smith notes that the front door is locked – even though Lane said it wasn't. He sees no sign of forced entry, by door or by window. There's a TV, a VCR, several guns in a closet, and other untouched items that would attract a thief. In her walkthrough, Jennings spotted a diamond wedding ring and other jewellery on a bedroom dresser. Jessie Lane's story of a burglar is sounding very shaky.

In the living room, Jennings and Smith notice an answering machine with the message light blinking. Jennings presses the button.

To everyone's shock, they hear Lane's voice say, "I'm sorry. I did it! I did it!" Clear and simple, he says he shot his wife. It's an accidental confession! How did his voice get on the tape? No one knows. Detective Smith wonders if Lane, being drunk, pressed the wrong button when he first tried to call 911.

Case closed? Not yet. Despite the taped confession, Lane insists he is innocent. The crime lab finds no fingerprints on the gun and no gunshot residue on Lane's hands. Jennings figures he washed his hands to clean off his wife's blood. But the crime lab does find GSR on his clothing.

In June 2006, a jury finds Jessie Lane guilty of murder, and a judge sentences him to 18 years to life in prison.

Forensic scientists who specialise in blood stains set up laboratory experiments to test how a spatter pattern likely formed.

Jewellery left untouched, in plain sight on top of a dresser, cast more doubt on Lane's story of a burglar. Even when jewellery is missing, though, investigators don't automatically jump to a conclusion of 'robbery'. Murderers sometimes steal items to make a crime scene look like a burglary.

21

ON THE CASE:

CRIME SCENE LOST

The moment a crime scene is found, there's only one chance to get it right, to properly document and process the scene. There are no 'do-overs' – no going back to fix mistakes. Why? Because processing a scene destroys it: the evidence will never be the same again.

What happens when a scene is contaminated – trampled, rearranged, or littered – before it is properly processed? The case of JonBenet Ramsey, a six-year-old girl from Boulder, Colorado, is a tragic example of what can happen.

At 9:30 p.m. on Christmas night, 25 December, 1996, Patsy Ramsey put her sleepy daughter to bed. Early the next morning, she went downstairs and was shocked to find a long ransom note. In the note, unknown kidnappers demanded $118,000 for the safe return of JonBenet.

Patsy Ramsey immediately checked the girl's bedroom and found that her daughter was missing. At 5:52 a.m., she called 911 emergency, and then several friends to tell them what had happened. With that phone call, the three-story house should have become a crime scene. Kidnappers had entered it. A little girl was missing.

Destroying the evidence

However, when police officers arrived, they failed to seal off the area. They failed to preserve and protect forensic evidence. They failed to search the house thoroughly. The Ramsey's friends arrived and walked around, freely, while Patsy Ramsey and her husband John waited for the kidnappers to call. (No one ever did.)

John Ramsey holds up a picture of his murdered daughter, JonBenet, at a press conference. Earlier, Patsy (left) had warned, "There is a killer on the loose . . . [and] if I were a resident of Boulder, I would tell my friends to keep their babies close to you."

Then, unthinkably, a detective asked John Ramsey and his friend to search the house for, 'anything unusual'. The men did so. Sadly, eight hours after the 911 call for help, Ramsey found his daughter, dead, in a basement room.

Investigators found hairs on the body that don't belong to Ramsey family members. But this physical evidence was collected after a parade of people had walked through the crime scene.

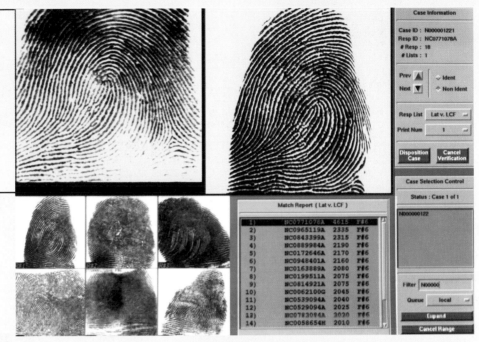

Fingerprints found at a crime scene can be entered into A.F.I.S, the Automated Fingerprint Identification System. This computerised database, set up by the FBI, automatically scans millions of prints for matches. Unfortunately, investigators found no useful fingerprints in the Ramsey house.

He removed duct tape from her mouth, picked her up, and carried her upstairs.

The house was finally declared a crime scene and everyone was cleared out. But it was too late. All hope was gone of properly collecting evidence from the body, the basement room, and the rest of the house and property. Any evidence that was found could too easily belong to someone other than the killer.

No answers

How did the killer get into and out of the house? Did he or she leave shoeprints going in and out of the basement room? Were there any fingerprints, hairs, fibres, DNA, and other trace evidence anywhere in the house? What was the exact position of the body as the killer left it? The answers to all those questions were compromised – made uncertain by the presence of people other than investigators at the crime scene.

As of October 2006, 10 years after the crime, the murder of JonBenet Ramsey remains unsolved. Even if police arrest a suspect, investigators might not be able to link the person to the compromised crime scene or victim. The lack of a direct, physical link, such as a DNA match, makes a 'guilty' verdict very tough to win.

Crime scientists processed DNA evidence from blood found on Jon Benet's clothes. The genetic material belongs to an unknown white male who is not a Ramsey family member. In 2003, the pattern was entered into CODIS, the FBI's computerised DNA database, in the hopes of finding a match.

Investigators use numbered markers to flag the location of blood drops, slugs, broken glass, and other evidence before they collect it.

Remember the first rule of forensic science? Every contact leaves a trace. But how do you find traces of evidence that are hidden, damaged, buried, microscopic, invisible, or scattered over a wide area? In fact, there were all of the above in one of the biggest crime scenes ever investigated. (See 'The Bombing of a Jumbo Jet,' page 30.)

Don't miss a thing

To find every shred of evidence, investigators set up search patterns that don't miss a thing. Note the phrase: every shred of evidence. It's impossible to collect and test every item at a crime scene. A C.S.I. has to decide what's evidence and what's not.

An investigator working alone can do a spiral search, walking the perimeter of the scene and circling inward toward the centre. A spiral search can also be done in reverse, from centre to perimeter.

A crime scene team can set up a line search: people stand shoulder-to-shoulder and baby-step or crawl forward in unison, eyes glued to the ground. If they spot something unusual, they don't pick it up. The searchers aren't always trained in handling evidence, so they don't want to join the chain of custody. Instead, they raise a hand or drop a marker, and a C.S.I. bags and tags the item.

Diane France of NecroSearch often organises line searches to look for the scattered bones of victims. The wilderness is crawling with bears, deer, and other creatures, who die and leave behind skeletons. So, as line searchers raise their hands, France runs up and down the line to check out each item. As a forensic anthropologist, she can tell at a glance if the item is a bone and, if so, a human or nonhuman one.

Eyes glued to the ground, police conduct a shoulder-to-shoulder, step-by-step line search for evidence. A sniper, a hidden sharpshooter, escaped from this crime scene after killing a victim.

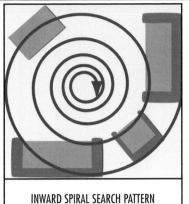

INWARD SPIRAL SEARCH PATTERN

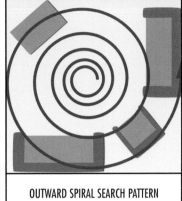

OUTWARD SPIRAL SEARCH PATTERN

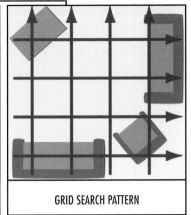

GRID SEARCH PATTERN

The third dimension

Line searches find evidence on the surface – the length and width of a crime scene. What about depth, the third dimension?

To uncover buried items, investigators set up a grid search. Using stakes and strings, they create a grid of one metre squares above the crime scene (see photo). Then, they dig into one square at a time, carefully removing the earth layer by layer. They use small shovels, chopsticks, tweezers, brushes, or other fine tools to avoid damaging evidence.

If they find something, they bag and tag it and note its exact location within the grid – which one-metre square, how far from the borders of that square, and how deep from the surface. The dug-up earth is sifted through screens to trap the tiniest clues – a button or a tooth, for example.

Using this grid system helps investigators create a three-dimensional picture of a crime scene, just as graph paper is useful for making a two-dimensional sketch. The picture shows exactly how one piece of evidence relates to another.

For example, in June 2006, NecroSearch found a grave without a body in a remote area. "The body was carried off by a bear," France says.

Among other questions, she wanted to know: what was the body's position when the killer left it? Was the grave dug quickly or carefully? (That's a clue to the killer's actions and habits.) What tools were used? What physical evidence was buried in the grave?

As the NecroSearch investigators removed layers of earth, they uncovered scrape

The NecroSearch team digs for evidence archaeology-style. Both crime scene investigators and experts on ancient objects use a grid system to map the location of found objects in three dimensions – length, width, and depth.

marks that showed the size and shape of the shovel. They found traces of decomposition – fatty acids and other body fluids that had leaked into the soil. They determined the size of the grave by marking where loose earth met compact, undisturbed earth. The one-metre grid squares provided exact positions for all this evidence – length, width, and depth.

Observing the invisible

Besides being scattered or buried, evidence can hide another way: it can be latent, or invisible. (Evidence you can see is patent.) If you're a fan of crime dramas, you know that chemicals and special lights make latent evidence appear – and sometimes glow an eerie blue that looks cool on TV.

Here's an old-fashioned example: fingerprint patterns are made of oil, protein, and sweat. Coloured powder brings out latent fingerprints simply by sticking to those substances. The investigator then photographs the print and lifts it with a piece of clear tape. The tape is stuck to a card, and the lifted print is sent to a crime lab for identification. (Everyone's fingerprints are unique. Even identical twins usually have different fingerprints.)

If evidence is invisible, how do you know where to look for it?

Sharon Plotkin, a C.S.I. in North Miami, Florida, uses observation and inference. Obvious places to start looking are entrances and exits – both doors and windows. As she observes the scene of a burglary, she asks herself: "Did the burglar eat? Drink? Use the bathroom? Move things? Interact with the pets? Cut himself?" Plotkin isn't present during the crime, of course, so she doesn't witness any of the burglar's actions. She has to infer them by clues left at the scene.

Inferring the unseen

If there's a dog in the home, perhaps the burglar petted the dog – and unknowingly took dog hairs from the scene. If those hairs are found on a suspect, they provide a direct, physical link to the scene of the crime.

Suppose a window or door lock has a tool mark – a dent, or scratch, or chip, left by a hard object. The inference is that the burglar made a forced entry, which means he or she was probably a stranger to the location. No sign of a forced entry indicates an 'inside job' – an employee of a business or a family member of a house owner.

Suppose shoeprints lead up to a patio window and stop in front of it. The inference is that the burglar peered inside, perhaps cupping two hands around the face to block out sunlight. That gesture leaves a 'karate chop' print on the glass – a latent print formed by the pinky-finger sides of the cupped hands. It's a good idea to dust that patio window at about head height (and to take photos of the shoeprints, of course).

Crime scene technician Sharon Plotkin dusts a mirror with coloured powder, hoping to reveal latent fingerprints.

THE C.S.I'.S INVISIBLE TOOLKIT

How can the well-equipped investigator make latent evidence appear? Here are a few of the many forensic science tools, with new ones always on the horizon.

This bathtub looks clean. But after a liquid chemical called Blue Star is sprayed on and the lights are turned off . . .

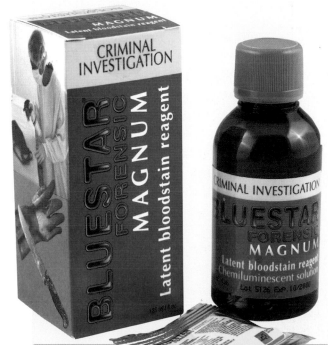

. . . a large blood stain glows brightly enough to show up in a photograph.

- Forensic lights shine ultraviolet (UV) or infrared light, in addition to visible light. These various frequencies of electromagnetic energy make bio stains either glow or darken. UV and infrared light are invisible to us, but some materials absorb this energy and then give off some of it at a frequency that we can see.

- There are dozens of other fingerprint chemicals and techniques. The choice of which to use depends on the age and content of the print (oily, sweaty, bloody, or high in iron) and on the surface (smooth or rough, porous, or watertight, and so on).

INSTANT WHITE DUSTING POWDER

DUSTING POWDER

DUSTING BRUSH

FINGERPRINT LIFTERS

FINGERPRINT CARDS

- Blue Star is one example of a blood reagent, a chemical that makes blood stains glow. It interacts with the iron in haemoglobin, so even if a stain has been wiped cleaned, washed with soap, or bleached. There are many other chemical reagents.

CRIMINAL INVESTIGATION

BLUESTAR FORENSIC MAGNUM Latent bloodstain reagent

CRIMINAL INVESTIGATION BLUESTAR FORENSIC MAGNUM Latent bloodstain reagent Chemiluminescent solution Lot 5126 Exp. 10/2000

27

DNA, DNA, DNA

With her search for bio, Plotkin is after much more than fingerprints, though. DNA is a molecule that's much too small to see without a very powerful microscope. Yet it's present in every body cell (except red blood cells). A strand of DNA contains sequences of chemicals unique to each person. More exact than fingerprints, DNA tests can match bio samples to individuals.

If a suspect drinks a glass of water or smokes a cigarette, there's DNA in the saliva left behind. If the suspect sheds a hair, or skin cells, or even the tiniest speck of blood, there's DNA in the bio. (Blood cells other than the red ones contain the DNA.)

Of course, criminals don't want to leave their DNA – or any evidence – behind. If they're smart, they don't help themselves to food and drink. They wear gloves to avoid leaving fingerprints. Some criminals work hard to clean up a scene – especially a bloody one in their home. But it's just as impossible for them to wipe away every trace as it is for a C.S.I. to find every trace.

Is It blood?

If a scene looks too clean, the C.S.I. can shine those eerie forensic lights that make unseen blood stains glow (see previous page). That's a clue to keep looking. The telltale glow is useless though, unless there's a stain that can be swabbed and tested for DNA and blood type.

A crime scene team in San Diego, California, entered a bedroom that looked spotless. After slow and careful searching, a detective finally found a spot – a dark red dot on the leg of a wood burning stove. She did a presumptive test for blood. To presume is to have a reason to believe something is true. A presumptive test proves whether it's true or not.

The detective used a chemical that reacts with the haemoglobin in blood and got a hit. She pulled back the carpet. The wood floor beneath it was scrubbed clean. Yet traces of blood had seeped between the planks. In the room below, the detective found a large pool of blood in the ceiling. So much for a 'spotless' crime scene! The owner of the house was convicted of murdering her husband.

A criminal wears gloves to avoid leaving fingerprints and DNA traces at a crime scene. But gloves make impressions on certain surfaces, and a single hair or skin cell or droplet of saliva can contain DNA.

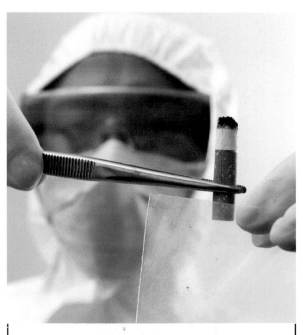

The saliva on a cigarette, the rim of a glass or cup, or a licked envelope can contain cells with DNA in them.

A CAREER IN CRIME SCIENCE
PROFILE: SHARON PLOTKIN, CRIME SCENE TECHNICIAN

Sharon Plotkin is a crime scene technician, but she isn't a police officer or a detective. She's a civilian who handles more than 300 cases per year in North Miami, Florida, a town of about 60,000 people.

Plotkin holds an advanced university degree in criminal justice, which is about the prison and court systems. She has taken hundreds of hours of classes in forensic science: in blood stain patterns, shoe impressions, gunshot residue, and other evidence techniques. Now, she teaches those skills to students. Plotkin handles most cases alone, investigating every crime except auto theft. "I don't want to sit behind a desk," Plotkin says. "Each day, I don't know what's coming." 'What's coming' isn't always pleasant. Plotkin doesn't mind the gore; she's used to it after 12 years on the job. But working a scene is often uncomfortable, to put it mildly. In more than one insect-infested home, she has tucked her trousers into her socks to keep out the bugs. "You can't have any fears," she says. "If you do, you have to work past them," she adds. She feels uneasy about heights, but she climbs on roofs to photograph crime scenes nonetheless. She used to be afraid of drowning. So she forced herself to take scuba diving classes. On one case, she collected casings – bits of metal from a street shooting – while lightning struck all around her. For her, the reward is solving a puzzle. Plotkin approaches each crime scene with the goal of making sense out of the chaos.

Her eye is so trained to details that it never stops looking. She can't go anywhere, including her own neighborhood, without thinking: "What's out of place? What doesn't belong here?"

With hundreds of cases under her belt, Sharon Plotkin shares her forensic science knowledge with students.

ALL THE LITTLE PIECES

With tape, tweezers, and other tools, C.S.I.s pick up tiny pieces of these and other trace evidence:

- Loose fibres from carpets, furniture, and clothing.
- Broken glass – especially car glass, which can be matched to the type of car.
- Flecks of paint, which are transferred from one object to another when a tool is used in a break-in or during a car crash, for example.
- Dirt or seeds or other pieces of ground, especially on tyres and shoes, which can link a suspect to a location.

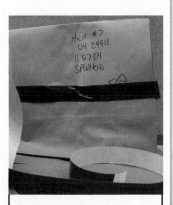

Sharon Plotkin sealed, signed, numbered, and labelled this evidence bag to start a chain of custody from crime scene to trial.

ON THE CASE:

THE BOMBING OF A JUMBO JET

On 21 December, 1988, shortly after 7 p.m., Pam Am Flight 103 exploded over Lockerbie, Scotland. The crash killed 270 people, including 11 people on the ground.

The wreckage and rubble spread 130 kilometres long and covered 2,189 square kilometres. In one of the biggest crime scenes to date, Scottish investigators and the F.B.I. set out to pick it all up.

Satellite images and helicopters helped spot items from above while volunteers on the ground did a fingertip search. They collected some four million pieces of debris!

Both wings, which carry the fuel, had burned up on impact. But investigators were able to rebuild the body of the aircraft. They found a hole about the width of a basketball hoop in the front cargo section. The material around it was blackened and badly damaged by a 'high-energy event' – a bomb, in other words.

A bomb explodes outward, in all directions, with a lot of energy. Much of that energy goes into propelling (throwing) objects at high speed. Near the bomb, tiny pieces of metal and other debris create a pitting pattern – little pockmarks that are a telltale clue to a bomb. Other pieces were blasted away in chunks. The nose cone, containing the cockpit, had landed on the ground in one piece.

Investigators picked through the mountain of debris, looking for blast damage and traces of explosive residue. They identified pieces of the brown suitcase that had held the bomb and a circuit board from a cassette player that was part of the bomb. Another circuit board fragment, found months later, was stuck in a piece of charred material.

Both fuel-filled wings, attached to part of the plane's body, crashed first, making a massive crater. Little remained of the plane parts and two homes. Eleven people on the ground died.

The most amazing clue to survive was a shred of baby clothing that had been wrapped around the bomb.

Investigators traced the second circuit board to the Libyan military and the baby clothing and suitcase to Malta.

In Malta, a store owner identified the Libyan who bought the clothing. In 2001, Abdel Basset Ali Mohamed Al-Megrahi, an intelligence agent, was found guilty of murdering 270 people. Another Libyan was acquitted.

Investigators pieced together as much of the plane's body as they could. They found a gaping hole on the left side where the bomb exploded.

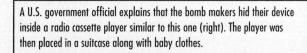

A U.S. government official explains that the bomb makers hid their device inside a radio cassette player similar to this one (right). The player was then placed in a suitcase along with baby clothes.

Second impressions

Fingerprints, DNA, and blood are the 'stars' of forensic science, making news headlines and playing the lead roles on crime shows. But Sharon Plotkin believes two other clues don't get enough credit: shoes and tyres.

"I'm the shoe queen," she says. "Criminals can wear masks and gloves, but until people learn to fly, they have to walk into and out of a crime scene." Cars, too, drive in and out.

Shoes and tyres pick up evidence – dirt, leaves, seeds, and other debris that a crime lab can sometimes link to a specific location. They also leave behind tracks called impressions.

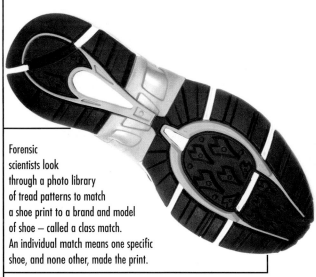

Forensic scientists look through a photo library of tread patterns to match a shoe print to a brand and model of shoe – called a class match. An individual match means one specific shoe, and none other, made the print.

Some impressions are flat outlines, like a dirty footprint on a patio or a skid mark on a road. These impressions can be latent or patent. Other impressions are three-dimensional: tyre tracks in mud or boot prints in snow.

C.S.I.s photograph all impressions and make casts – solid copies – of the three-dimensional ones. To make a cast, they pour in a liquid called plaster of Paris, wait for it harden, and then lift out the block. The cast shows the pattern of the impression in reverse – dents become bumps and vice versa.

Following the footprints

Crime lab experts work hard to match shoeprints to shoes and tyre tracks to tyres. It takes a highly trained forensic scientist to estimate shoe size based on a print.

At the crime scene, the C.S.I. observes and follows footsteps to figure out the criminal's actions: how many people were present? Were they running or walking? What paths did they take through the scene? Where did they slow down, stop, or change direction? Do the footprints have materials, like mud or grass, that can be traced to another location?

Sometimes, footprints lead C.S.I.s to the suspect's exit route – and to a whole new crime scene to investigate.

Rain washes away the details of shoe prints, but muddy tracks are still useful clues. They can lead to another crime scene or to hidden evidence – a dumped weapon, for instance.

Investigators cast impressions made in soft dirt using a casting compound. When the cast sets it can be transported to a crime lab.

Before this cast of a shoe print hardened, the investigator wrote the date on top.

ON THE CASE:

IF THE SHOE DOESN'T FIT

A set of shoeprints landed George McPhee in prison for murder.

On 24 September, 1984, he and Colin Hawkins were robbing homes on Black Isle, Scotland. One of them ran into the house of Elizabeth Sutherland and, surprised to find someone at home, murdered her. Each man accused the other of the crime.

Detectives found four running shoeprints in the soft soil outside and dirty shoeprints inside the home, on a carpet near the body.

Hawkins wore a size 7 or 8 shoe. McPhee wore a size 9. A detective testified that the prints were size 9 or 10 and that the crime lab had confirmed that number. The trouble was, the crime lab actually found it was 'impossible' to pinpoint the size. When you run in soft soil, your foot slips, pushing dirt back a little. The print is bigger than the shoe. Also, you land on the ball of your foot, further distorting the impression.

The lab report was withheld from the trial.

McPhee was found guilty and served 18 years before the report came to light. He was freed in 2003, and a court 'quashed' the conviction in 2005.

One bloody shoe print contains a boon of clues: the size and style of shoe, the gait (pausing, walking, running), the direction headed, and more. Investigators can also test a suspect's shoes for matching blood.

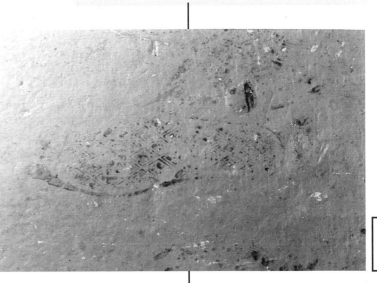

After processing a crime scene, an investigator writes a report that lists the evidence collected.

At the heart of the report is a narrative, a story-like description of events. The narrative doesn't explain what the C.S.I. thinks about the crime. It explains what the C.S.I. observed and did at the scene. It sticks to the facts of "What happened here?" The crime scene report helps detectives form a theory of the crime.

What is evidence? What is not? Investigators ask that question, again and again, at every crime scene. Ordinary items like a lemon can take on extraordinary meaning at a trial.

The evidence speaks

In writing her reports, Sharon Plotkin lets the evidence tell the story.

"I don't want any facts ahead of time," she explains. "No witness statements, no background. I look at the crime scene first and let the evidence speak."

If she sees a knife with a stain, she doesn't think, "That's the murder weapon." If she did, and she turned out to be wrong, she might overlook the real weapon. Instead, she photographs the knife, does a presumptive blood test, and bags it for the crime lab. Then she keeps observing with an open mind.

Plotkin doesn't focus on witness statements for this simple reason: "People lie. I don't want to be taken into a direction by a lie."

One witness told police he cut himself while chopping fruit. Plotkin

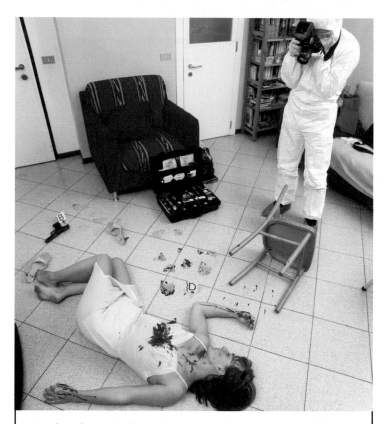

A trainee learns how to take forensic photos at a staged crime scene. 'Point and shoot' isn't good enough. The C.S.I. has to know about film speed, lenses, lighting, angles, shutter speed, and other technical details.

A C.S.I. uses notes, measurements, sketches, and photos to reconstruct the crime scene on a computer. The position of the body and the path of the bullet, shown by a yellow arrow, indicate where the shooter was standing.

found exactly one piece of fruit, a lemon, unchopped, at the crime scene.

"I took a zillion photos of that lemon!" she says.

Criminals lie because they don't want to get caught, of course. They also sometimes stage the crime scene: they plant evidence to point the finger of guilt at someone else. They steal a watch and a wallet to make a murder look like a bungled robbery.

Fortunately, they're usually bad at it. Experienced C.S.I.s can see through those tricks. They see the evidence for what it is.

Can you? On the next page is a crime scene report adapted from the facts of a real case. It's a case that makes you wonder, what kind of thief steals 'really ugly' art?

WHAT'S A THEORY?

Detectives rely on the crime scene report, an autopsy report (if there's a body), lab results, witness statements, and other evidence to form a theory of the crime. But what is a theory?

- A theory states who did it, the motive (why), the method (what and how), and the place and order of events (where and when).

- Remember, this is crime science, so detectives use the word theory in a scientific sense. A scientific theory is not 'just an idea,' as many people mistakenly believe. It's not a guess about what happened – not even an educated guess. And it's not an opinion or a point of view. A scientific theory is an explanation of events that fits all the known facts.

- There are always unknown facts in an investigation. So, any new evidence that comes to light will either support the theory or prove it wrong.

- Good detectives change their theory to fit the facts, rather than look for facts to fit a theory.

As the fictional detective Sherlock Holmes says, "It is a capital mistake to theorise before one has data. Insensibly one begins to twist facts to suit theories, instead of theories to suit facts."

ON THE CASE:

THE 'REALLY UGLY' PICASSO

Los Angeles, California, home to Hollywood movies, is one of the few cities with an Art Theft Detail in the police department. Two detectives work full-time to track down tens of millions of dollars in stolen art – along with the thieves who steal it.

This crime scene report was adapted from one of their case files. Read it carefully, and then think like a detective:

• What evidence is important?

• How do the witness statements relate to the evidence?

• What do you observe about the shoeprint?

• What can you infer about the broken window?

• What is the likely point of entry?

• What does the evidence say about the motive and method of the burglar?

• What's your theory of the crime, based on the known facts at this point in the investigation?

Crime Scene Report

West Los Angeles Police Department

Location: Large estate of a movie producer in West Los Angeles, California (name and address withheld for privacy)

Date of report: Saturday, 30 December, 2000

Crime: Burglary

Items reported missing: Faune drawing by Pablo Picasso, three Picasso plates, two bronze sculptures, a Tiffany lamp.

Total estimated value: $205,000

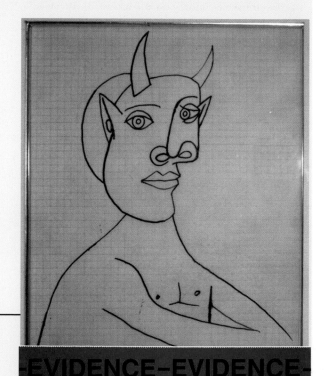

-EVIDENCE-EVIDENCE-

A thief thought Picasso's Faune drawing was 'really ugly' but stole it anyway. A faune is a Roman god in the shape of a man with the horns and tail of a goat.

This door leading into the kitchen was found closed, unlocked, and with a broken window pane.

Witness Statements and Background

The property manager of the estate said the owners were out of town. On the morning of Friday, 29 December, he discovered a cracked windowpane on a back door. While checking the house, he noticed items were missing.

The owner employs 29 fulltime workers, including maids, cooks, nannies, gardeners, a driver, and others.

The head gardener stated the timed sprinklers near the side door were set to turn on at 4:00 a.m. on Mondays, Wednesdays, and Fridays.

The security company reported that no alarm activated.

The main gate of the property is massive and cannot be climbed over. To enter with a car, the suspect had to punch an access code into the security system. There is a parking area at the top of a hill.

The windowpane next to the door knob on the back door was cracked but intact. It bulged out at the centre (see close-up photo page 37).

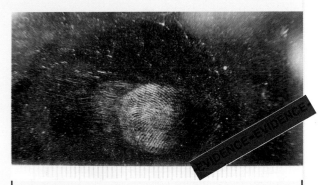

A fingerprint was lifted from a side door that showed no sign of forced entry.

The door was closed and reportedly unlocked at the time of discovery (Friday morning). It opens into the kitchen.

Muddy shoeprints led to a side door that opens into a pool table room.

Photographs were taken and casts were made of the shoeprints.

One quality latent fingerprint was lifted from the glass on this door.

The door showed no sign of forced entry.

The alarm system was not working properly.

The Tiffany lamp and two bronze sculptures had been in the pool table room. The Picasso artwork had been in the living room.

Footprints appear to go directly to the items taken. Many additional items of equal or greater value were not stolen.

There was no ransacking (reckless searching through drawers and closets).

Turn to the next page to read the detective's theory, and to find out how the case was cracked...

The cast is a negative impression of a shoe print – dents become bumps and bumps become dents.

ON THE CASE:

CONCLUSION TO: THE 'REALLY UGLY' PICASSO

Who stole the movie producer's valuable art? It wasn't a stranger. But that's about all Detective Don Hrycyk (her–RIS–ik) knew for sure based on the crime scene evidence. He and his partner in Art Theft Detail took over the case on 3 January, 2001.

The Cracked Window

About the cracked windowpane, Detective Hrycyk told a reporter, "That was dumb." The thief had tried to kick it in, but a plastic coating kept it from falling to pieces. The window bulged, but it didn't break open. A small hole in the centre wasn't large enough for a hand to pass through and unlock the door from the outside.

The 'dumb' part was the direction of the bulge. It showed the thief had kicked the window from inside the house!

The detective reported, "Entry was made with a key through a side door by a possible employee. The suspect staged a phony forced entry at the back door to make it appear as if a stranger had committed the crime."

If not a stranger, who did it?

No match was found for the fingerprint, but that evidence was of limited value. The estate had at least 29 full-time employees on any given day. Many of them had keys and were free to walk around. Their fingerprints were all over the estate.

Detective Hrycyk focused his attention on the side door, the point of entry.

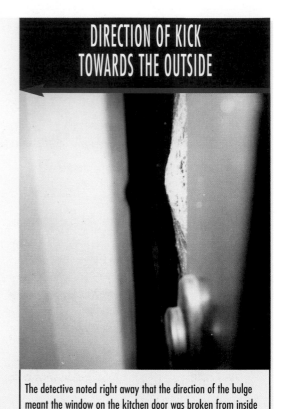

DIRECTION OF KICK TOWARDS THE OUTSIDE

The detective noted right away that the direction of the bulge meant the window on the kitchen door was broken from inside the house.

The muddy shoeprints

Large muddy shoeprints, with thick treads, led directly to the door. The detective wondered, "When was the ground muddy?"

ART THEFT CASE

The sprinklers went on and off at different times. The ones near the side door had turned on Friday morning at 4 a.m., a few hours before the property manager checked the house.

Based on the evidence, the detective narrated the order of events: the burglar parked his car on a hill, walked across a muddy area, used his key to open the side door, and entered the pool table room. The burglar grabbed the lamp and statues, walked to the living room, stole the Picassos, and then entered the kitchen.

The brand and model of the suspect's boots is a class match to the tread pattern of the shoe impression at the scene.

for several reasons. But no direct evidence linked Archer to the crime. Archer said he didn't do it.

Nabbed in the act!

On 3 May, 2001, a man named Tony Hargain tried to sell what he called 'a really ugly drawing' to an auction house. It was the Faune Picasso drawing, listed as stolen. The security chief called Detective Hrycyk, who set the trap.

When Hargain pulled the drawing out of his car trunk, thinking he had a buyer, police arrested him. The man's real name turned out to be Sammie Archer III!

Archer had a list of 10 art dealers where he had tried to sell stolen goods. The detective tracked down each one to gather witness statements.

Archer's home had a size 12 Timberland boot that was consistent with the muddy shoeprints.

The art thief pleaded guilty to burglary, grand theft, and receiving stolen property. He was sentenced to one year in jail.

There, he unlocked the door and kicked the windowpane to stage a fake forced entry.

Because he grabbed items at hand, bypassing those of greater value and not stopping to ransack, the motive was clearly money, and not a love of art. The burglar intended to sell the goods, which were now listed in a 'Stolen Art' computer database.

Detective Hrycyk talked to the estate owner, who suspected his driver, Sammie Archer III,

ART THEFT CASE

CASE CLOSED

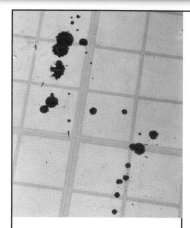

Observing and measuring blood drops is pure science, but interpreting what they mean is partly an art.

Detective Christine Kruse-Feldstein, a C.S.I. in Miami-Dade County, says it takes 40 minutes to log one gun into evidence. There's the log book, which lists line after line of evidence for every case. There's the chain of custody – the list of people who take charge of the gun. There are more forms to request lab tests and for the ATF, the US government agency in charge of guns.

All this paperwork, all the strict rules, all the slow and careful searching and collecting have a purpose: to make sure the evidence stands up in court.

Beyond a doubt

Mistakes can keep evidence out of a trial or allow the defense lawyer to create doubt about a person's guilt. Suppose there's a time, even a few minutes, when no one has official custody of a gun in evidence. A defense lawyer can suggest someone tampered with it during that time – even switched it with another gun. Jurors then think, "What if that's true?" There's a seed of doubt.

No case is ever 100 percent certain. But, at the end of the trial, if there's reasonable doubt, a jury has to say, "Not guilty." Reasonable doubt means the jury can't say with confidence and conviction that the person is guilty. But it's a slippery definition. Many trials slide one way or another unpredictably. (See 'A Mountain of Evidence?,' page 42.)

The chain of custody rule for handling evidence is like passing a baton in a relay race. One person hands it directly to the next, never dropping or losing it, all the way to the finish line – a trial verdict.

One piece of evidence is almost never enough to convict a criminal. A tyre track can prove someone's vehicle was at a crime scene. But when? Was it at the time of the crime or before or after? And who was driving?

WHAT CAN EVIDENCE DO?

Physical evidence proves that someone is guilty by linking a suspect to a crime scene, to a victim, or to another piece of evidence – like a weapon. But evidence does much more than that. It can also:

- Prove that a crime happened.
- Reveal events that took place at a crime scene ("What happened here?").
- Help detectives build a time line of events.
- Identify a nameless corpse.
- Support or not support what a witness or suspect says.
- Rule out innocent people as suspects.

'by the book,' and other mistakes. When C.S.I.s testify in court, they have to answer some tough questions about the quality of their work. Nichol Jennings says the key is to stay on top of your game.

"If you're thorough about the evidence, careful with notes, and have a record of everything, you feel confident when you testify. You know your stuff. You're on top of it!"

A forensic expert is scraping off paint transferred onto this car by another vehicle that hit it. The chemistry of the paint is unique to a make (for example, Ford), model (for example, a Mondeo), and sometimes year, which narrows the search for the hit-and-run suspect.

ON THE CASE:

A 'MOUNTAIN OF EVIDENCE'?

Los Angeles prosecutor Marcia Clark believed the crime scene team had collected a 'mountain of evidence' against O.J. Simpson. In 1995, the ex-American football star went on trial for the murder of his ex-wife, Nicole Brown Simpson, and her friend, Ronald Goldman.

In a media blitz, it became the 'Trial of the Century'. But back to that 'mountain of evidence,' Here are a few peaks.

Crime Scene: Nicole Brown Simpson's House

• Both Nicole Simpson and Goldman were brutally stabbed to death. The scene was awash in blood, but of special interest were a few drops on her back. An investigator took a close-up picture of them. Because they were on her back, they more than likely belonged to the killer or had dripped off the murder weapon.

The gated front entrance to Nicole Brown Simpson's Los Angeles home was awash in blood. Her body was found at the base of the steps.

On 17 June, 1994, O.J. Simpson, age 46, went from American football superstar to double-murder suspect.

• Bloody shoeprints leading away from the body were made by very expensive, size 12 shoes. This was O.J. Simpson's size and he had owned the brand, though no such shoes were found in his home.

• A trail of dripped blood had O.J. Simpson's DNA. He had a cut on his finger, but gave several explanations as to how he got it.

• O.J. Simpson's blood was also found on the gate and

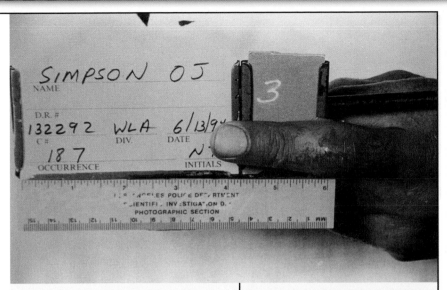

several other places at the scene.

- Hairs consistent with O.J. Simpson's were in a knitted cap next to Goldman's body.

Crime scene: Simpson's vehicle and estate

- A bloody right glove, matching the left glove found at the scene of the crime, was recovered from the property. DNA in the blood matched all three parties – the two victims and O.J. Simpson. There were also fibres from Goldman's shirt and hair from both victims.

- Drops of blood were found in the driveway, bedroom, and bathroom.

- Two bloody socks were found in the bedroom. The DNA matched O.J. and Nicole Simpson.

- The vehicle, a Ford Bronco, had blood stains from all three parties. O.J. Simpson had never met Ron Goldman.

The day after the murders, detectives noted three deep cuts on the middle finger of Simpson's left hand. Were they knife wounds or from shattered glass, as Simpson claimed?

Not guilty?

Keep in mind this is only part of the evidence. Then hold onto your hat while you think this over: a jury found O.J. Simpson not guilty.

Turn the page to find out what went wrong with the evidence.

The head juror (who has been elected by the jurors to speak for them) reads out a verdict at the end of a court case.

Turn the page to find out what went wrong with the evidence.

WHO'S IN COURT?

- A defendant is the person on trial for a crime.

- A prosecutor is a lawyer who tries to prove that the defendant is guilty. A guilty verdict is the same thing as a conviction.

- A defence lawyer defends the defendant. He or she seeks a 'not guilty' verdict, also called an acquittal.

- A jury is a group of 12 citizens (in a criminal case) who listen to all the evidence and decide on the verdict.

THE TRIAL OF THE CENTURY: BY THE NUMBERS

- Simpson's defence lawyers: 11

- Los Angeles prosecutors: 9

- Witnesses who testified: 150

- Reporters covering the trial: about 2,000

- Length of trial: 9 months

- Cost of trial: £7–£10 million

ON THE CASE:

A 'MOUNTAIN OF EVIDENCE'?

Johnnie Cochran, the leader of Simpson's 'Dream Team' of lawyers, told the jury that the evidence was "contaminated, compromised, and ultimately corrupted."

Cochran set out to prove that investigators made crime scene and lab mistakes and planted evidence on purpose to make Simpson look guilty. In other words, there were plenty of valleys (low-points) in the 'mountain of evidence'.

Crime scene:
Nicole Brown Simpson's house

- The coroner wasn't called to the scene until many hours later.
- The bodies were moved before trace evidence – fibres from the clothing and hairs – were collected.
- An investigator covered Nicole Simpson's body with a blanket to discourage photographers. The blanket left fibres, which mixed with the evidence on her body.
- Nicole Simpson's body was turned over, and she was put in a body bag before samples were taken of the drops of blood on her back. No one will ever know whose blood that was.
- Vials of blood evidence weren't carefully counted and logged in at every stage. The chain of custody was broken.
- Some blood evidence was found and collected days or weeks after the murder.

Crime scene:
O.J. Simpson's home

- The socks had evidence that the blood was planted on them. The blood contained a chemical added to samples to preserve them, but that is not found in the human body.

- A vial of O.J. Simpson's blood was missing a small amount.
- A detective carried around blood evidence in an unsealed container for three hours.
- Not all the blood evidence collected was challenged. But a defense lawyer explained, "Once you conclude that the blood on the sock was planted, you begin to have doubts about all the rest of the evidence."
- At trial, Simpson tried on the pair of gloves, but couldn't get them on. Cochran told the jury, "If it doesn't fit, you must acquit." However, Simpson was wearing rubber gloves on his hands when he tried on the leather gloves.

Another trial, another verdict

O.J. Simpson was acquitted of murder in the criminal trial. But the Goldman and Brown families sued him in a civil case. Civil cases are about money paid for wrongs done. They don't require proof beyond a reasonable doubt. The proof is a 'preponderance of the evidence' – enough evidence to make it likely that Simpson was responsible. The families won their case, and the court ordered Simpson to pay them millions of dollars.

MURDER CASE

CASE CLOSED

The 'C.S.I. effect'

What happens when a crime scene investigation is done right? Here's a simple example:

Bruce Richenthal shot his parents and tried to make it look like a murder-suicide. He laid the bodies side-by-side and placed the gun in his mother's hand. Detectives knew right away the scene was staged for a number of obvious reasons. For example, the mother's legs were partly off the bed as if trying to escape. Detectives suspected the son, who denied it and claimed he wasn't home at the time of the crime.

Sharon Plotkin nailed Richenthal by doing a slow and detailed search of the entire crime scene. In his room, inside his closet, she looked through every pocket, every bag, every shoe. When she picked up a sneaker, she heard a rattle. Inside, she found a piece of tooth belonging to the mother! It was a 'smoking gun' – key evidence that linked a killer directly to a crime beyond a reasonable doubt.

Richenthal was convicted of double murder. C.S.I.s always hope for just such a magic moment, but they know it's rare. More often, they round up a variety of evidence, not all of it direct or clear-cut.

In what's called 'the C.S.I. effect,' many jurors expect more certainty. They watch popular crime dramas like the *C.S.I.* and *Law and Order* series. Then, they think real cases should be solved like the TV cases: in a short time, by high-tech and flawless science, and with a 'smoking gun' found at the last second. As a future juror, beware of the 'C.S.I. effect'. Enjoy these shows, but know that they are fiction. They sometimes even make up the 'science' altogether! Want the truth about crime scene investigations? Read about real people working real cases with, more often than not, imperfect endings.

Sharon Plotkin (top) and Christine Kruse-Feldstein at work. A real crime scene can take days to investigate, all the while remaining under guard by police until the slow, careful job is complete. All that hard work doesn't always result in a conviction.

A PERSON OF SCIENCE

If the law has made you a witness
remain a person of science
you have no victim to avenge
no guilty or innocent person
to convict or save
you must bear testimony within
the limits of science and let the
evidence speak for itself

Dr. P.C.H. Brouardel, 19th Century,
French Medico-legalist

Glossary

biological: Having to do with living organisms. Investigators called it 'bio' for short.

civilian: A person who is not in the military or on a police force.

conviction: a guilty verdict.

custody: The state of being held, detained, or safeguarded. When police make an arrest, the suspect is 'in custody'.

cyanide: A deadly chemical that kills by depriving body cells of oxygen.

detective: A member of the police force who investigates cases and solves crimes.

DNA: A molecule that's present in every life form and contains sequences of chemicals that form the 'code of life' – the genetic instructions for making a plant, animal, or other organism. The letters stand for DeoxyriboNucleic Acid.

evidence: Proof or disproof. It can be physical (blood, or a weapon) or testimonial (witness statements).

forensic: Having to do with evidence in an investigation – a crime, an accident, a natural disaster, and so on.

forensic scientists: People who collect, process, and analsze evidence in a criminal case. They can be detectives or civilians and often specialise in the crime scene, fingerprints, blood spatter, DNA, ballistics (guns and bullets), impressions (tyre tracks and shoeprints, mainly), tool marks (made by weapons), or other areas.

haemoglobin: A blood protein with iron in it. Oxygen molecules (O_2) in the lungs attach to the iron in haemoglobin and are carried throughout the body by the blood stream.

homicide: A manner of death in which one person kills another. Murder is the most serious type of homicide. It can also be manslaughter (a less serious charge) or assisted suicide (helping someone die on purpose).

inference: An indirect observation.

latent: Invisible, as in latent fingerprints. Visible evidence is patent.

magnetometer: A remote-sensing device that detects and measures magnetic fields, which are created by the presence of iron, for example. Magnetic fields in the soil align north-south, like a compass, unless disturbed.

molecule: Atoms bonded together, as in H_2O water, which is two hydrogen atoms and one oxygen atom.

projectile: An object that's propelled or thrown, including a bullet.

reagent: Any substance that's used in a chemical reaction. A blood reagent is any chemical that causes a reaction in blood – makes the haemoglobin protein glow, for example.

testify: Answer questions under oath in a court of law.

case files, view pictures of stolen art, see if you can tell real masterpieces from fake ones, and more. *www.lapdonline.org/art_theft_detail*
CourtTV's Forensic Files:
A database and case files of forensic investigating techniques – fingerprints, DNA, hair and fibre evidence, and so on.
http://www.courttv.com/onair/shows/forensicfiles/glossary/1.html
The FBI's Page for Kids: Activities and games from the Federal Bureau of Investigation, the U.S. government office that investigates federal crimes.
http://www.fbi.gov/kids/6th12th/6th12th.htm
Who Dunnit?: Online, fictional cases for you to crack.
http://www.cyberbee.com/whodunnit/crime.html

BOOKS

Mystery stories are a great way to learn how to think like a detective, especially the cases of Sherlock Holmes, written by Sir Arthur Conan Doyle. These books, below, are nonfiction guides.
The Forensic Casebook: The Science of Crime Scene Investigation, by N.E. Genge (Ballantine, 2002). This detailed text is peppered with the true tales of C.S.Is, detectives, and other experts. The sections on crime science careers and training are excellent.
Forensics, by Richard Platt. (Kingfisher/Houghton Mifflin, 2005). How to process a crime scene, measure ballistics (bullets and other projectiles), tell counterfeit money from real money, and more.
Detective Science: 40 Crime-Solving, Case-Breaking, Crook-Catching Activities for Kids, by Jim Wiese (Jossey-Bass, 1996). How to collect trace evidence, lift fingerprints, make tooth impressions, and other hands-on activities.

WEBSITES

Access Excellence's The Mystery Spot:
Online or downloadable fictional mysteries for you to solve that rely on science.
http://www.accessexcellence.org/AE/mspot/
The Art Theft Detail unit of the LAPD: Read more

Publisher's note to teachers and parents:
Our editors have carefully reviewed these Web sites to ensure that they are suitable for children. Many Web sites change frequently, however, and we cannot guarantee that a site's future contents will continue to meet our high standards of quality and educational value. Be advised that children should be closely supervised whenever they access the Internet.

Index